BOATS ON A RIVER

Julie Marie Myatt

BROADWAY PLAY PUBLISHING INC
New York
www.broadwayplaypublishing.com
info@broadwayplaypublishing.com

BOATS ON A RIVER
© Copyright 2019 Julie Marie Myatt

Cover photo: Julie Marie Myatt

First edition: November 2019
I S B N: 978-0-88145-813-8

Book design: Marie Donovan
Page make-up: Adobe InDesign
Typeface: Palatino

BOATS ON A RIVER was commissioned by the Guthrie Theater (Artistic Director, Joe Dowling) as part of the Guthrie New Play Program funded by the Bush Foundation.

BOATS ON A RIVER had its world premiere at the
Guthrie Theater in Minneapolis, running from 19 May–
10 June 2007. The cast and creative contributors were:

TED THOMPSON ....Peter Christian Hansen
SIDNEY WEBB ....Nathaniel Fuller
SISTER MARGARET ....Dale Hodges
JONATHON BLACK .... Kris L Nelson
YEN ....Jeany Park
LIDA ....Mayano Ochi
KOLAB....................................... Rebecca J Wall
MAX SENG.....................................Randy Reyes
TAM WEBB.....................................Yoko Fumoto
CAMBODIAN GIRLS ..... Aeola Lu, Megan K Mecklenburg,
                     Anna Northenscold, Isabelle Yang

Director.......................... Michael Bigelow Dixon
Set design.....................................Victor A Beker
Costume design........................... Lynda K Myers
Lighting design.........................Matthew Reinert
Sound design........................ Reid Rejsa
Video design................................Heidi Edwards
Dramaturg................................... Amy Wegener
Voice & dialect coach .... Elisa Carlson
Movement ....Stuart Pimsler
Video images .... Carol Banker & Julie Marie Myatt
Stage management..............................Jody Gavin
Assistant stage management ....Amy Monroe
Assistant director............................Steve Moulds
Dramaturgy intern ....Katie Schoeneck

CHARACTERS

SIDNEY WEBB, *late 40s, early 50s. American. Been in Cambodia since 1992. Started the after-care center. Ministry background.*

SISTER MARGARET, *early 60s. British. Nun. Has lived all over the world, working with children.*

JONATHON BLACK, *early 30s. American. Human Rights Lawyer. Idealist. This is his first assignment.*

MAX SENG, *late 20s. Psychologist. Cambodian, raised in the United States.*

KOLAB, *5 years old. Cambodian. (To be played by young actress, not 5 year old)*

LIDA, *8 years old. Cambodian. (To be played by young actress, not 8 year old)*

YEN, *13 years old. Vietnamese. (To be played by young actress, not 13 year old)*

TED THOMPSON, *mid-30s. American. Clean-cut. On vacation to Cambodia for the first time with his new video-camera.*

TAM WEBB, *mid-30s. Vietnamese.* SIDNEY WEBB's *wife. Well-dressed, poised and beautiful.*

Two Cambodian girls

SETTING

Place: city of Phnom Penh, Cambodia
An after-care shelter for girls freed from sex slavery.
Time: 2007

ACT ONE

(As the audience enters, Cambodian pop music plays and they find the three girls, KOLAB, LIDA, YEN, *standing on stage. Bored. Waiting)*

(One by one, the girls are beckoned off stage…by routine, they slip out of their shoes and exit to different dark corners. It's time for them to go to work.)

(However, as the lights fade, they are not women's shoes that remain on stage where the women once stood, but three tiny pair of children's pink sandals.)

Scene 1

(Video:)

*(*TED THOMPSON *holds the video camera up to record his own face.)*

(He remembers to smile.)

TED: Ted Thompson here. Uh. April 12, 2007. *(Looks at his watch)* Four forty-five A M. Guess we can call this Day 1. Of, of my big trip…. Uh… Traveling light. One bag packed and ready to go…. Uh. Butterflies in stomach. Passport in hand. Destination—

WOMEN'S VOICE: *(O S)* Honey?

TED: Yeah?

(Video stops.)

Scene 2

(SIDNEY WEBB's *office. Phnom Penh*)

(*Evening*)

(SISTER MARGARET *gathers the kids shoes from the stage.*)

(SIDNEY *sits quietly over a cup of tea. Both are exhausted. There are children's drawings hanging from every surface of* SIDNEY's *office wall.*)

SIDNEY: English Breakfast?

SISTER MARGARET: I think so. Yes.

(*Silence*)

SIDNEY: Your sister send it?

SISTER MARGARET: Brother.

SIDNEY: He's a good guy, your brother.

SISTER MARGARET: Sure.

SIDNEY: Charles. The dentist. Where's he live again?

SISTER MARGARET: Australia.

SIDNEY: Left London?

SISTER MARGARET: Yes.

SIDNEY: Where in Australia?

SISTER MARGARET: Melbourne.

(*Silence*)

SIDNEY: Nice town, Melbourne.

SISTER MARGARET: Yes.

SIDNEY: You've been there?

SISTER MARGARET: No.

SIDNEY: What's the population there, you think?

SISTER MARGARET: I don't know.

SIDNEY: He like it there?

SISTER MARGARET: Why are you so interested in my brother all of the sudden?

SIDNEY: I don't know.

SISTER MARGARET: Go home.

SIDNEY: You so rarely talk about yourself.

SISTER MARGARET: You're not asking about me.

SIDNEY: Well, inadvertently I am.

SISTER MARGARET: Why should I go on about myself (or my brother in Melbourne) when you should have been home with your wife and kids hours ago.

SIDNEY: I don't know, I just—

SISTER MARGARET: Go. Home.
(She sets the shoes down in an orderly row.)

(SIDNEY drinks more tea.)

SISTER MARGARET: Sidney?

SIDNEY: What?

SISTER MARGARET: Why do you do this?

SIDNEY: What?

SISTER MARGARET: Neglect your wife.

SIDNEY: I'm not neglecting her.

SISTER MARGARET: What do you call this?

SIDNEY: Working.

SISTER MARGARET: We're not working.

SIDNEY: Exhaustion.

SISTER MARGARET: Not too exhausted for, "this is good tea—what kind is it—where'd you get it—what's the population of the world—I want to know more about you and your brother—Margaret, talk to me, spill your heart out about Melbourne—".

SIDNEY: It's late. She's asleep now anyway.

(SISTER MARGARET *stares at* SIDNEY.)

SISTER MARGARET: I'm going to start counting and I want you out of here and on your way home to your wife, by three.

SIDNEY: Your iron fist doesn't work with me.

SISTER MARGARET: One… Two…I'm serious.

SIDNEY: I'm sure you are.

SISTER MARGARET: You're a terrible husband.

SIDNEY: What if I went around telling you, you're "a terrible Catholic"?

SISTER MARGARET: Am I?

(Silence)

SIDNEY: I have a hard job—

SISTER MARGARET: It's so disappointing.

SIDNEY: I have a lot of responsibilities.

SISTER MARGARET: Go home and please stop with the excuses…I still haven't said three…you still have a chance…I'm still counting…I won't harm you if you get up in the next second…three—

(SIDNEY *stands. Sighs*)

SIDNEY: I'm going.

(SIDNEY *opens the door and* JONATHON BLACK *enters smiling.*)

JONATHON: Mr Webb?

(It takes SIDNEY *a moment to realize that his opening the door was an invitation.)*

SIDNEY: Yes.

JONATHON: I'm Jonathon Black.

SIDNEY: I'm sorry…

JONATHON: We spoke on the phone. I'm a lawyer.

SIDNEY: A lawyer…

JONATHON: We spoke on the phone last week--I'm here with a human rights group from the United States called "Action for All".

SIDNEY: Right. Right.

JONATHON: Yes. Nice to meet you.

SIDNEY: "Action for All."

JONATHON: Yes. I like your place—

(SIDNEY *shakes* JONATHON's *hand.*)

SIDNEY: It's a little late for office hours—

JONATHON: It's very, quaint—

SIDNEY: And I thought you were coming next month.

JONATHON: We were. But we've planned a raid for tonight.

SIDNEY: Tonight?

JONATHON: Yes, sir. We thought this would be a more effective way to start.

SIDNEY: Why?

JONATHON: No one knows we're here.

SIDNEY: I see. So you've been in Phnom Penh…

JONATHON: Five days. Undercover—

SIDNEY: And you are going to raid a brothel in—

JONATHON: Roughly…sixty-two minutes.
(*Silence*)
We want to catch them off guard. (Obviously.) Less chance for the pimps and police to talk. Exchange money. Bribes. And so forth. It's all extremely well-planned. Extremely.

SIDNEY: Uh huh.

JONATHON: We know what problems exist here, so we're going to come out of no where.

SIDNEY: You're coming out of no where.

SISTER MARGARET: Was this your idea, young man?

JONATHON: *(Trying to hide his pride)* Yes, ma'am. Actually. It was.
(He holds out his hand to SISTER MARGARET.)
Jonathon.

SISTER MARGARET: Yes.

JONATHON: Black…

SISTER MARGARET: How many girls?

JONATHON: In the brothel?

SISTER MARGARET: Please.

JONATHON: Oh…well, we think twenty-five or so.

SIDNEY: Twenty-five?

SISTER MARGARET: Or so.

JONATHON: Roughly twenty-five. We don't have an exact number.

SIDNEY: That's a lot.

JONATHON: And they need our help. This is what "Action for All" is all about.

SISTER MARGARET: What?

JONATHON: I'm sorry, ma'am--what do you mean, what?

SISTER MARGARET: What's it about, this "Action for All"?

(JONATHON tries to hand SIDNEY and SISTER MARGARET a pamphlet from the organization.)

JONATHON: "Rescuing victims of exploitation, saving women and children from sexual slavery, and keeping vulnerable communities from the hands of human traffickers and harm's way."

SIDNEY: Where—

JONATHON: "All over the hemisphere. All over the globe."

SISTER MARGARET: Hemisphere and globe?

JONATHON: We got it covered.

SIDNEY: Where are you going to put them?

JONATHON: Who?

SIDNEY: These "twenty-five or so" girls.

JONATHON: Here.

SISTER MARGARET: We're full.

JONATHON: It would be temporary.

SISTER MARGARET: We don't have room.

JONATHON: But I told Mr Webb on the phone—

SIDNEY: And if I remember correctly, I told you then we were already exceeding our capacity.

JONATHON: Well, we have to take them somewhere, and we've heard you have the best facilities.

SIDNEY: We do. But it doesn't change that we don't have space for twenty-five more girls. Much less the two infants that Margaret and I just delivered.

JONATHON: Don't you have a doctor on hand—

SIDNEY: There wasn't time.

JONATHON: Well, sorry, I've called every N G O in the city and they said your shelter had to take them.

(Silence)

SIDNEY: Where are you from, Mr Black?

JONATHON: Texas.

SIDNEY: The great state of Texas.

JONATHON: Yep.
(Trying to lighten the mood)
Don't mess with it.

SIDNEY: Oh, it's messing with me.

SISTER MARGARET: Sidney, we can't—

SIDNEY: What time do you think your well-planned, undercover, top secret mission will conclude?

JONATHON: We should be back here with the girls, hopefully, oh, let's say, around four-thirty.

SIDNEY & SISTER MARGARET: A M?

JONATHON: Yes.

SIDNEY: Four-thirty A M. Have you dealt with children before, Mr Black?

JONATHON: Yes. Of course.

SIDNEY: Have children of your own?

JONATHON: No.

SIDNEY: Married?

JONATHON: No.

SIDNEY: So, you've—

JONATHON: My brother has two boys.

SIDNEY: Uh huh.

JONATHON: And I was a psych major.
(Silence)
And I have a law degree from Georgetown. Please. I assure you, Mr Webb, I've been training for this very mission for—

SISTER MARGARET: Do you speak Khmer?

JONATHON: Cambodian?

SISTER MARGARET: Khmer. Yes.

JONATHON: Of course. A little. Enough.

(SIDNEY *and* SISTER MARGARET *share a look.*)

JONATHON: Look. I know what I'm doing. We've trained for this—Action for All has a very high standard, extremely high—

SIDNEY: Please... Let me just get this straight. I'm sorry. I'm a little tired. Delivering twins from a underfed fifteen year old is harder than you'd think. Okay. So. You are going to pull twenty-five "or so" frightened, screaming girls from a brothel—

SISTER MARGARET: Some of whom now consider that their home, and some of whom, only speak Vietnamese, I might add, not Khmer—

SIDNEY: And you are going to bring them here, at four-thirty in the morning, for us, a staff of two on hand at the moment, I can't call in our other workers because I promised them the night off, so the two of us, Sister Margaret and I have to try and calm and attend to and find a place for them to sleep—

SISTER MARGARET: And they won't want to sleep really, because they are used to being up at night, much of their lives happens at night, as you might imagine—

SIDNEY: And so now they'll wake up all thirty of the other girls who have just gotten used to the quiet nights of this shelter, just begun to feel safe, and just as they are feeling safe and secure in our care, twenty-five "or so" hysterical girls—

SISTER MARGARET: Some whom have S T Ds, or —

SIDNEY: Are going to come barreling in simply because you tell me you studied some psychology, got a degree from Georgetown, your brother has kids, and, this is going to be a great success because you've been in Cambodia five days and "Action for All" knows what it's doing.

JONATHON: Yes.

(Silence)

SIDNEY: Well. Great. Go to it, Mr Black. Sister Margaret and I will be waiting.

SISTER MARGARET: We don't have room—

SIDNEY: I guess we'll have to make room, won't we. Mr. Black's from Texas. We better accommodate him.

(JONATHON isn't sure what to do.)

(He finally takes that as a cue to exit.)

SISTER MARGARET: Where are we going to put twenty-five girls—

SIDNEY: I don't know.
(He is looking around his office.)

SISTER MARGARET: Sidney?

SIDNEY: What?

SISTER MARGARET: We don't have room.
(Silence)
You should have gone home.

SIDNEY: Why?

SISTER MARGARET: I would have told him no.

SIDNEY: I did tell him no.

SISTER MARGARET: But you didn't mean it.

SIDNEY: Yes I did.

(Silence)

SISTER MARGARET: Your wife is a patient woman.
(Silence)
Call her.

SIDNEY: I will.

SISTER MARGARET: Sidney?

SIDNEY: What?

SISTER MARGARET: Call her and tell her you're not coming home—

SIDNEY: It's too bad you're a nun.

SISTER MARGARET: Why?

SIDNEY: You'd make a terrific wife.

(SISTER MARGARET hands SIDNEY the phone.)

SIDNEY: I probably married the wrong woman.

SISTER MARGARET: Don't flatter yourself.

SIDNEY: Why?

SISTER MARGARET: You're not my type.

SIDNEY: What's your type?

SISTER MARGARET: The type that can say no.
(She exits.)

(SIDNEY dials.)

Scene 3

(Video:)

(The camera is turned toward TED in his seat on the airplane.)

TED: Ted Thompson. On the plane. En route. Little nervous. Never been on a flight this long. Uh. But it appears there are some good in-flight films to look forward to. That should make the time speed by. Several meals. Another time killer…I have pre-ordered the vegetarian meals, of course.

(Next to him in the seat is JONATHON.)

TED: I'm sitting next to…

JONATHON: Jonathon.

TED: Jonathon. Destination Phnom Penh?

JONATHON: Yes.

TED: How's your trip going so far?

JONATHON: Fine.

TED: Traveling for business or pleasure?

JONATHON: Business.

TED: Pleasure… First time in Asia. First time overseas, actually.

JONATHON: Really?

TED: Decided I'd take my two-weeks vacation and do something exotic this year. Do something really memorable for once, you know?

JONATHON: Sure.

TED: Cross the Pacific into the East. The great unknown. The wild.

JONATHON: Uh huh.

Scene 4

(SIDNEY's office)

JONATHON: (O S) Oh no… Please… This way…this, this way… Hands to ourselves… Please…this way please… this way…

(Lights up on three girls, YEN, KOLAB, and LIDA. And JONATHON. He looks like hell, but tries to keep a smiling face on for the girls.)

JONATHON: We'll just, we'll just wait in here.

(YEN, defiant, stands in the middle of the stage, trying to use the phone.)

JONATHON: Oh. No. Please don't touch that. Please. Please don't touch anything in here—it could be

private. Or important—please don't touch the
telephone.

(KOLAB *stands in the corner of* SIDNEY'*s office, alone and
frightened.*)

(LIDA *sits nervously behind the desk. She picks up a framed
photo.*)

JONATHON: And and, no no, please don't touch that.
It's not yours—

(YEN *reaches for the phone again.*)

JONATHON: No. No. Please. Don't. Really. Now…
please.

(*He moves it away from* YEN.)

I think, I think I just said to you, please, please don't
touch the telephone.

(YEN *touches it with one finger.*)

(JONATHON *just looks at her.*)

JONATHON: I see you know what touch means.

(YEN *tries to pick up the telephone, but* JONATHON *beats her
to it.*)

JONATHON: I did say please.

(JONATHON *and* YEN *stare at each other. [Her staring
makes him uncomfortable.]*)

JONATHON: Do you know what "please" means?

(*More staring*)

JONATHON: Who are you going to call, one of those
pimps? The police? You really think they care about
you?

YEN: (*Quietly*) Fuck you.

JONATHON: You know, where I come from, those words
really are considered not very lady like. I don't know
who taught you that—

(To LIDA*)*
—hey, you, you over there, please don't touch that—
(He sets down the phone.)
I believe I already asked you once…I really don't
like to repeat myself…please don't touch that photo
again, you're getting finger prints on it and it could be
important—

*(*YEN *picks up the telephone.)*

JONATHON: Please. Now put down that telephone!—
please—there will be no calls tonight! —No telephones
will be used!—

*(*JONATHON *and* YEN *are both pulling on the telephone
as—)*

*(*SIDNEY *and* SISTER MARGARET *enter, each holding a
sleeping baby.)*

SIDNEY: Mr Black. Well now. Hello. The guards told us
you were here.

JONATHON: Hi.

*(*SIDNEY *checks his watch.)*

SIDNEY: And look at that—you are, four-thirty on the
nose. Bravo.

JONATHON: *(As he yanks away the telephone from* YEN*)*
I've really tried to keep your office in order but it's
been impossible. These girls want to touch everything.

SIDNEY: Huh.

JONATHON: You do something nice for them and still
they don't listen.

(This stops SIDNEY.*)*

JONATHON: I hope nothing's ruined.

*(*SIDNEY *decides to let it go.)*

SIDNEY: It's fine.

(He passes a glance to Sister Margaret *and turns his attention to the girls.)*

Sidney: Svaakohm... Niak ch'muah ei?

(They stare at Sidney.*)*

Sidney: Does my Khmer sound funny to you?

(They nod.)

Sidney: I know you're scared, but no one will hurt you here.

(They continue to stare.)

Sidney: And I'm sorry...
(To Jonathon*)*
We don't like shouting. Shouting is scary.
(To Lida*)*
Isn't it? ...Do you want to look at the baby?

*(*Lida *touches the baby's face.)*

Sidney: Sweet, isn't she?

*(*Lida *nods.)*

Sidney: My name is Sidney. This is Sister Margaret.

Sister Margaret: Welcome.

Sidney: And I think you've already met the famous Mr Jonathon Black.

*(*Lida *nods.)*

Jonathon: You, you can just call me Jonathon——

Sidney: *(To* Lida*)* What is your name?

Lida: Lida....

Sidney: Lida. Very pretty name.

Lida: She is Kolab.... And she is Yen.

Sidney: Very nice to meet you, Lida. Kolab. And Yen.

(They don't respond.)

SIDNEY: Sister Margaret will take you to get some tea and something to eat.

(They look at JONATHON.*)*

SIDNEY: It's okay. Margaret, you want to take these girls to the kitchen now?

SISTER MARGARET: What about the baby—

SIDNEY: Hand her to Mr Black, and he'll make sure she doesn't wake up. He's very good with children.

JONATHON: What—

*(*SISTER MARGARET *reluctantly hands the sleeping baby to* JONATHON.*)*

SISTER MARGARET: Mind her head.

SIDNEY: I'll see you in the morning, girls.

SISTER MARGARET: It's alright. Come along.

(They slowly stand and follow SISTER MARGARET. YEN *looks at* KOLAB *and* LIDA, *then looks the men over, and follows* SISTER MARGARET *off stage.)*

*(*SIDNEY *watches* JONATHON *grow uncomfortable with* YEN's *staring.)*

SIDNEY: Where are the rest of the girls?
(He looks around the room.)

JONATHON: Oh. Well.
(He clears his throat.)
Well. You see…

SIDNEY: Sssh—
(He sways the baby in his arms.)
What happened?

*(*SIDNEY *encourages* JONATHON *to watch how he's holding the baby…)*

JONATHON: There, there was a problem.

(JONATHON *watches* SIDNEY, *and now sways the baby in his arms in the same calming fashion.*)

SIDNEY: What kind of problem?

(Silence)

JONATHON: There was a little, a little chaos during the raid.

SIDNEY: What kind of chaos?

JONATHON: Kind of chaos… Kind… Well. Uh. Let's see. We broke through the door and everyone started running and screaming, and then the pimps were so fast, they were rounding them up and they took off in a van, and the next thing we knew, everyone was gone and all we had were these three girls sitting at our feet, crying.

SIDNEY: And?

(Silence)

JONATHON: It was awful.

(Silence. Together, in unison, JONATHON and SIDNEY men sway the sleeping infants in their arms.)

JONATHON: I've never seen conditions like that. I mean, it's one thing to hear about it, and, to read about it. I've seen the documentaries. I felt extremely prepared, I did, but to see it, first hand…the conditions they have these girls…I just…all these young girls, locked inside like hens in a hen house. Stale air. Life shut out from the inside. Five, six year olds…teenagers, clinging to each other. Little shoes everywhere… Pink and red sandals…tiny tiny shoes… Left beside doors… Doors to…dark rooms. Secret corners. Or curtains. Nothing but curtains dividing some places. And they see us come in with guns and start running into hallways, doorways, scatter and…screaming. Everyone was screaming.

(Silence)

JONATHON: It was a mess.

(Silence)

And you knew it would be. Does that give you some kind of pleasure?

SIDNEY: It doesn't give me the slightest bit of pleasure.

JONATHON: Why didn't you tell me?

(Silence)

SIDNEY: If I had a nickel for every American I've seen come through this country and leave shaking their heads... They just don't get it. Things function differently here.

JONATHON: I know—

SIDNEY: This is not the West.

JONATHON: I know—

SIDNEY: It's not a wild ride over the Panhandle at dawn.

JONATHON: I never thought it was—

SIDNEY: Just because you sneak up on a place doesn't mean they can't outsmart you.

JONATHON: We were well-organized.

SIDNEY: And you think they're not?

(Silence. JONATHON finally really looks at the baby in his arms.)

JONATHON: Where's their mother?

SIDNEY: Sleeping.

JONATHON: Is she going to keep them?

SIDNEY: I don't know. I haven't asked her that.

JONATHON: Huh.

(Silence)

They're cute.

SIDNEY: Yeah.

JONATHON: Where are they going to sleep?

SIDNEY: With their mother—

JONATHON: No. I mean the girls I brought in tonight. Where are you going to put them?

SIDNEY: In here, I guess.

JONATHON: Here?

SIDNEY: Looks like it. For a few days anyway—

JONATHON: They're going to sleep in your office?

SIDNEY: You got a better idea?

JONATHON: Well—

SIDNEY: Now you're worried where the girls are going to sleep? What's going to happen to them? ... What about the other twenty-two you sent screaming? Where do you think they're sleeping tonight?
(Silence)
Hand me that baby.

(JONATHON awkwardly hands the baby over.)

SIDNEY: Welcome to Cambodia, Mr Black.
(He exits.)

(JONATHON sighs, takes in the children's drawings with unsure interest.)

JONATHON: Thanks.
(He slowly exits.)

Scene 5

(Video:)

(The streets of Phnom Penh through a taxi window. Motor bikes everywhere. Dust)

TED: *(O S)* Day 2. Arriving into Phnom Penh. Ted Thompson in a taxi. Made it in one piece. That guy Jonathon talked my fucking ear off and I missed half the good movies on the plane. And he hogged the arm rest…. But I'm not going to dwell on that…that was then, this is now…I'm in the now now.

(Shots of billboards and street life.)

TED: *(O S)* All eyes are open to the Kingdom of Cambodia…. Look at that…huh…lot poorer than I expected…huh… Well.

(The sights zoom past - mixture of growth and Third World—cars and ox carts, etc.)

TED: *(O S)* Let the adventure begin.

Scene 6

(SIDNEY's office)

(SISTER MARGARET hands out pillows and blankets to KOLAB, LIDA, and YEN.)

SISTER MARGARET: Alright, my little angels. Here's your room. Find a spot on the floor and try and get some sleep. We'll help you get settled in the morning.

(The girls stand staring at SISTER MARGARET.)

SISTER MARGARET: There's nothing to be frightened of. It's just an office. I know it's messy and not very cozy, but it's quiet. And safe.

(More staring)

LIDA: *(Whispers to* YEN*)* What did she say?

YEN: She doesn't speak Khmer.

LIDA: What is she speaking?

SISTER MARGARET: I'm speaking Khmer.

YEN: You are?

SISTER MARGARET: Yes.

YEN: Sounds funny.

SISTER MARGARET: Well, of course it sounds funny. I'm English.

LIDA: Where's that American man?

SISTER MARGARET: Which one?

LIDA: What?

SISTER MARGARET: Which American man?

LIDA: The nervous one.

SISTER MARGARET: Don't you worry about him.

LIDA: I don't think I like him.

SISTER MARGARET: You girls need to get some sleep.

LIDA: I'm not tired.

SISTER MARGARET: I didn't ask if you were tired, did I?

LIDA: I don't know.

SISTER MARGARET: What do you mean, you don't know.

LIDA: I only understand every other word you say.

SISTER MARGARET: It's not an easy language.

LIDA: Yen learned it.

SISTER MARGARET: She's a smart girl then, isn't she?

YEN: Too smart to be stuck in here.

SISTER MARGARET: Don't start with that talk.

YEN: What talk? Talk Khmer lady!

SISTER MARGARET: I'm talking Khmer!

(LIDA *and* YEN *giggle.*)

SISTER MARGARET: The old lady is so funny.

YEN: She sounds like a chicken.

(*The girls giggle some more.*)

SISTER MARGARET: Alright. Very funny. Ha ha ha Laugh at the chicken lady. Now lay down and close your eyes, my silly gigglers.

LIDA: Why?

SISTER MARGARET: Because we've got five new angels in the shelter today, including you three, and if I am going to take care of you, I need to get my beauty rest.

LIDA: What did she call us?

YEN: Angels.

LIDA: Why?

YEN: Probably thinks it makes us feel good.

SISTER MARGARET: You are good.

YEN: That's what the men say.

SISTER MARGARET: Is that right? Is that what they say about you?

YEN: Yes.

SISTER MARGARET: I'm sorry to hear that.

YEN: Why?

SISTER MARGARET: Look at all of you, smart, lovely girls…. You can do many many things…I'm sure of it… You'll see…. Are you alright there, my quiet Kolab? Can I make you a little bed on the floor? Nice and cozy?

(KOLAB *backs away from her.*)

SISTER MARGARET: No? …You take your time then. Settle in. Welcome to your new home angels. We're glad you're here. Sleep tight. Mind the bed bugs don't bite.

(SISTER MARGARET *turns out the lights and exits.*)

LIDA: What are they going to do to us?

KOLAB: Someone turn on the lights.

LIDA: Don't be a baby.

KOLAB: I'm not being a baby. It's too dark.

LIDA: Turn on the lights then.

KOLAB: I can't.

LIDA: Why not?

KOLAB: It's too dark. You do it.

LIDA: No.

KOLAB: Why not?

LIDA: I don't want to.

KOLAB: C'mon. Please.

LIDA: No.

KOLAB: Why not?

LIDA: It's too dark.

(YEN *turns on the lights.*)

YEN: You're both babies.
(*She pulls a cigarette from inside her dress.*)
And don't get any ideas. I'm not going to take care of you like some big sister or mommy or dumb aunt. If you two have a problem, deal with it yourselves. I'm not your baby-sitter.
(*She also pulls out a box of matches, and one chipped tea cup.*)
You're on your own.

(She reaches for the phone.)

*(*SISTER MARGARET *enters. Takes the cigarette from* YEN.
Unplugs the phone and takes that too)

SISTER MARGARET: God bless you.

*(*SISTER MARGARET *turns off the lights again, and exits.)*

Scene 7

*(*SIDNEY's *office. Night)*

*(*YEN *paces.)*

*(*LIDA *and* KOLAB *sit with eyes open.)*

Scene 8

*(*SIDNEY's *office. Later)*

*(*LIDA *paces.)*

*(*YEN *and* KOLAB *sit with eyes open.)*

Scene 9

(Video:)

(Shot of TED's *bright hotel room.)*

TED: *(O S)* Just woke up from a four hour nap…
Jet lag… Whew. Wipe out…. But I've got a nice
room. Overlooks the Mekong river. Lots of bars and
restaurants. Uh, everything's certainly affordable. I've
got A C. That's a plus. A must, actually. It's hot. Really
hot.

Scene 10

(SIDNEY's office. *Morning*)

(YEN *and* LIDA *sleep.* KOLAB *sits awake in the corner.*)

(*She sits staring at the walls around her.*)

(SISTER MARGARET *enters with the telephone.*)

SISTER MARGARET: Good morning, my little sunshines.
(*She plugs it back in, and notices* KOLAB *in the corner.*)
What's wrong over here? Huh? …What's the matter?
(*Silence*)
What's the matter then…you can tell me…it's alright.

KOLAB: I miss my mamma.

SISTER MARGARET: Maybe you'll be able to see her
again someday—

KOLAB: She's going to be angry.

SISTER MARGARET: Maybe not—

KOLAB: Yes.

SISTER MARGARET: Why?

KOLAB: We didn't run.

(*Silence*)

SISTER MARGARET: That woman is not your mother,
sweetheart. You don't have to worry what she thinks
now.

KOLAB: I'm not going to see her?

SISTER MARGARET: No.

KOLAB: Ever?

SISTER MARGARET: No.
(*This is devastating news.*)
Your real mother might like to see you again.

KOLAB: No.

SISTER MARGARET: She might.

KOLAB: No—

YEN: Her real mother sold her.

SISTER MARGARET: That's not kind, Yen.

YEN: What about you? Telling her she won't see Mamma again.

SISTER MARGARET: That woman—

YEN: Took care of her.

SISTER MARGARET: And made a lot of money doing it.

YEN: What do you want?

SISTER MARGARET: You girls need a good meal. A new start on the day.

YEN: What do want from us, lady?

SISTER MARGARET: I want you to meet all the other girls who live here.

YEN: No thanks.

SISTER MARGARET: Why not?

YEN: I'm not staying.

SISTER MARGARET: Why don't you come meet the other girls and see how they feel.

YEN: Why can't I leave?

SISTER MARGARET: Because we want to help you.

YEN: Why are there locks on the gate?

SISTER MARGARET: To protect you.

YEN: From?

SISTER MARGARET: Those greasy pimps that circle the block three times a day.

YEN: Really?

SISTER MARGARET: Yes.

LIDA: That's what Mamma said.

SISTER MARGARET: What?

YEN: That the locks were to protect us.

SISTER MARGARET: Well, maybe we're both trying to protect you. But from different things.

YEN: What makes this any better?

SISTER MARGARET: No one will be having sex with you here.

YEN: So you say.

SISTER MARGARET: It's the truth.

YEN: Then why are we locked in?

SISTER MARGARET: I told you—

YEN: What if the three of us walked up to the front door to leave, what would happen?

SISTER MARGARET: Why don't you come eat some breakfast before you plan on leaving.

YEN: I'm asking you.

KOLAB: What's for breakfast?

SISTER MARGARET: Eggs and toast.

KOLAB: I've never had that.

YEN: You didn't answer my question.

SISTER MARGARET: I'm hoping that you won't want to leave.

YEN: I'm not as little as these two.

SISTER MARGARET: I know.

YEN: I should be able to make up my own mind.

SISTER MARGARET: You should. But I am hoping that I might change your mind.

YEN: What for? What do you want?

SISTER MARGARET: We want to help you.

YEN: Why?

SISTER MARGARET: Because we care about you.

LIDA: Are you going to let us go home later?

SISTER MARGARET: I'm trying to explain to you, this is your new home, for awhile—

LIDA: I don't like it here.

SISTER MARGARET: How do you know you don't like it here?

LIDA: I don't know where I am.

SISTER MARGARET: Come to breakfast. When was the last time you had a good, hot breakfast?

YEN: We're not dogs. You can't bribe us with food.

SISTER MARGARET: I'm not trying to bribe you, darling, I'm trying to give you some food for your stomach. So you'll be healthy. Strong. Feel better.

YEN: Same thing.

SISTER MARGARET: It's not the same. I promise you that, sweetheart. Not the same at all. Come on now, let's go. Follow me.

(They reluctantly exit as SISTER MARGARET *nudges them off stage.)*

LIDA: Could you just tell me where I am?

Scene 11

(Video:)

(Shot of a land mine victim walking down the sidewalk)

TED: *(O S)* Six P M. Day 4. Huh… Room service is good. I had some rice and curry. Spicy. I liked that… Uh…I haven't left my room. Not yet… I'm hesitant. I feel nervous. I don't know why. Maybe it's the heat. I just...I don't know.

Scene 12

(SIDNEY's office.)

(SIDNEY *hangs up phone and finds* YEN's *chipped tea cup among his things. He picks it up to examine it as* MAX SENG *enters.*)

SIDNEY: These last twenty-four hours have been a fucking nightmare. We got some hotshot American guy with his idiot "Action for All" group that's causing more trouble in town than goddamn carnival. I got three calls at home this morning from other shelters complaining that the police have got their panties in a bunch because no one told them this new group was coming in town. The police themselves called six times. Some woman, I've never met, just called wanting to take the twins with her to the United States in the morning (the Action for All asshole met her in his hotel lobby and gave her my fucking number) because she and her husband just bought a new four bedroom house in the Chicago suburbs and invetro didn't work, thousands of dollars later, and she wanted to assure me that they could provide the best home for them with their wall-to-wall carpeting and three-car garage, and excellent school district, shit...I'm tired, we're overcrowded, and my wife wants to separate.
(*Silence*)
How are you?

MAX: You need to speak to a shrink.

SIDNEY: I thought I was.

MAX: I mean one of my friends... Someone who's not so familiar.

SIDNEY: No.

MAX: Why not?

SIDNEY: I don't have time.

MAX: That's no excuse—

SIDNEY: I don't have time.

(MAX *takes a piece of paper from* SIDNEY's *desk, writes down a phone number, and hands it to* SIDNEY.)

MAX: Call him. He's good.

SIDNEY: Have you seen the twins yet? They're pretty healthy considering—

MAX: Sidney?

SIDNEY: What?

MAX: This place can't afford for you to have a melt down.

SIDNEY: I'm not going to have a melt down.

MAX: Famous last words at the peak of self-destruction—

SIDNEY: I'm fine.

MAX: Really?
(*Silence*)
What did you tell your wife?

SIDNEY: I thought it was a good idea.

MAX: And what did she say?

SIDNEY: I think she was hoping for a different response.

MAX: So what are you going to do about it?

SIDNEY: I—

(YEN, LIDA, *and* KOLAB *enter with* SISTER MARGARET.)

SISTER MARGARET: Good morning. Three full bellies.

SIDNEY: Morning. Did you get proper introductions at breakfast, girls?

SISTER MARGARET: We were a little shy.

SIDNEY: Well, that's natural.

MAX: Of course.

SIDNEY: Girls, I'd like you to meet Max. He's our psychologist. He's going to take a moment to speak to you all individually. Learn a little more about you.

LIDA: Alone?

MAX: Sister Margaret can sit with us, if that would make you more comfortable.

LIDA: Where are you going to take us?

MAX: Out in the garden. We can just have a seat under one of the trees and talk.

(The girls look at each other.)

LIDA: What do you want us to do?

MAX: Talk.

YEN: How much?

SIDNEY: Max helps people talk about their feelings. I promise he has no other intentions.

YEN: Sure.

SIDNEY: Tell you what, you can all go out to the garden and watch as each of you speaks to Max. That way you know it's safe, alright?

MAX: If you don't want to talk, you can draw. Do you girls like to draw?

YEN: You all talk to us like we're children.

MAX: I'll make sure I talk to you like an adult.

(The three girls stand still.)

SISTER MARGARET: It's alright, girls. It's a lovely day. All the other girls are outside… Go on.

(MAX *leads them off stage.* YEN *lags behind.*)

YEN: Do I have to?

SISTER MARGARET: I think you might like talking about yourself.

YEN: Why?

SISTER MARGARET: You're interesting.

(YEN *takes her tea cup from* SIDNEY's *desk.*)

YEN: *(Mumbles)* This place is stupid.
(*She exits.*)

SIDNEY: How was breakfast?
(*Silence*)
Margaret?

SISTER MARGARET: They huddled in a corner. By themselves.

SIDNEY: That's not unusual—

SISTER MARGARET: The young ones ate quietly, while Yen stared at a wound on her arm…I think she has AIDS.

Scene 13

(*Video:*)

(*Shot of moto, taxi, and tok tok drivers approaching camera.*)

TED: (O S) No thank you…no…no thank you…no…no thank you.

(*Shot of people crossing in front of camera at riverfront.*)

TED: (O S) Day 5. Ted Thompson had to get outside. But I'm not sure what to do next.

(Shot of monks walking, kid running with stick, girl running in water.)

TED: *(O S)* I don't know what I was expecting.

(A woman sleeps in the curve of a sign stand.)

(Shot of little boy jumping beside his mother, digging through trash.)

TED: *(O S)* It's a lot dirtier here than I thought it would be.

(The little boy looks at the camera, the camera follows him.)

TED: *(O S)* Hey there little buddy.

(The little boy smiles and stares.)

(Shot of mother and daughters, a toddler plays in the street, grabbing a tin can.)

TED: *(O S)* Everything feels so...reckless.

(Video images of Phnom Penh continue to play silently through the next three scenes.)

Scene 14

(YEN and KOLAB sit on one side of the stage, watching. There are several dolls and blocks on stage.)

(MAX sits taking notes on:)

(LIDA sits in a chair in the center of the stage, playing with the hem of her dress, telling her story.)

LIDA: I am eight years old. My birthday is in July. I am from Battanbang Province. My father died when I was five years old. He was a very good man with long eyelashes and big ears. My mother is a small woman who is not strong. She has a mole on her cheek. She loves her family and she tries to feed us but is not good at working in the fields like my father. Her body is too small. I have two older sisters and two brothers. My

brothers are younger than me. One day, my aunt asked my mother if she wanted her to take me and my sisters to the city to go to school and live with her. My mother was sad but said yes, we could go to the city, because we were all hungry and poor, because my brothers needed her more. My mother cried when we left but we were excited to see the city. I was excited. I wanted to go school. But my aunt did not take us to live with her. She took us to an older woman who lives in a big house. She never told us her name. She had a lot of furniture inside her house. Silk pillows and rugs on the floor. She had a car outside. She had two guards. She was rich. She gave my sisters and me a Coke to drink with a straw. That was the first time I had that kind of sweet drink and I liked it. The bubbles felt like they were dancing in my mouth. It made me laugh because that felt so strange. My oldest sister asked for another and the woman gave us all another Coke to drink. This older woman had a little brown dog. I don't remember his name. He was friendly to us. From the big house I went in a car. Just me. It came to pick me up. Just me. The driver never turned around to look at me. Even when I asked him where we were going. He kept driving. I don't know where my sisters went. I have not seen my sisters since that big house. I don't know where they are but maybe they are still there with the dog and the old woman who gave us Coke drinks…
And that's it.

MAX: Thank you, Lida. You're very good at expressing yourself.

LIDA: Do you think she lives near here?

MAX: I don't know—

LIDA: She might—

(KOLAB *reaches for a doll* LIDA *has been holding—*)

KOLAB: Can I see this now?

MAX: Lida?

(LIDA *hands the doll to* KOLAB.)

MAX: Do you want to tell me about yourself, Kolab?

(KOLAB *walks away with the doll.* MAX *follows.)*

MAX: Excuse me, Lida…

LIDA: *(Mumbling)* She could live down the street from here…

Scene 15

(KOLAB *is fascinated by the doll. She is distracted by it. Undressing it. Pulling on it's legs. Its arms)*

(MAX *sits with her, waiting.)*

(Waiting)

MAX: Will you tell me about yourself, Kolab?

(Silence)

(KOLAB *continues pulling on the doll.)*

Scene 16

(YEN *slumps in the chair, her legs swinging nervously, but more seductively than most 13 year-olds.)*

YEN: Is this your job?

MAX: Yes.

YEN: Staring at people?

MAX: My job is to listen to you. Talk to you. Sometimes that involves staring.

YEN: What if I don't want to talk about me?

MAX: What would you rather talk about?

(YEN *shrugs, keep swinging her legs.)*

YEN: Leaving.

MAX: That's a short subject. Seems kind of boring to me.

YEN: You sound weird.

MAX: My Khmer sounds weird?

YEN: Kinda.

MAX: I learned it from my parents. I was raised in America.

YEN: Why'd you come here?

MAX: I'm Khmer. This is my home.
(*Silence*)
You said you are thirteen?
(*Silence*)
How long have you lived at Svay Pak?

(YEN *shrugs.*)

MAX: You don't know?

YEN: Since I was eight.

MAX: Eight years old. And you came from Vietnam?

YEN: Apparently.

MAX: Your Khmer is very good, you know. Perfect.

(YEN *shrugs.*)

MAX: You don't like compliments, Yen?

YEN: They're fine.

MAX: How did you get from Vietnam to Svay Pak?
(*Silence*)

YEN: How everyone gets from Vietnam to Svay Pak.

MAX: How is that?

YEN: Without anyone knowing.

MAX: Knowing what?

YEN: The secret roads. The secrets of the Mekong River. The secret armies and police.

MAX: How do you know it's a secret?

YEN: *(Whispering)* Everyone tells us to be quiet. No one has papers. Everyone speaks in quiet voices and threatens in quiet voices.

MAX: What do you remember about it?

(YEN shrugs again.)

YEN: I slept.

MAX: Were you given something to make you sleep?

YEN: I guess so.

MAX: What was it?

YEN: A little pill.

MAX: Who gave it to you?

YEN: A man.

MAX: Did you know him?

YEN: No.

MAX: Did he make you take it?

YEN: He didn't make me but I did.

MAX: Were you afraid of him?

YEN: I was eight.
(She stops swinging her legs.)

MAX: I'm sorry… That must have been scary for you… everything new and unfamiliar and—

YEN: Kind of like this?

MAX: Maybe… Do you miss your family, Yen?

YEN: Do you miss yours?

MAX: Yes. Do you miss yours?

YEN: Do you have any candy here?

MAX: No.

YEN: Do you ever have candy?

MAX: Yes. Sometimes.

YEN: When?

MAX: On special occasions... Where in Vietnam is your family?

YEN: I don't know.

MAX: Were you on your own?

YEN: What do you mean?

MAX: Were you living on the streets?

YEN: I guess.

MAX: How did you feel about that?

(YEN shrugs.)

MAX: Do you want to go back to Vietnam?

YEN: No.

MAX: How do you feel about being here, in the shelter—besides you want to leave?

YEN: I think it's stupid.

MAX: What makes it stupid?

YEN: What do you want us to do here?

MAX: Be safe. Get a chance to get out of the sex trade.

YEN: And do what?

MAX: Have a better life.

YEN: This doesn't look much better to me. It's boring. *(She flops in her chair with boredom. Touches the wound on her arm)*
And you don't have candy.

MAX: Can I see your arm?

YEN: Why?

Scene 17

(Video:)

(Night in Phnom Penh. Moto bikes zoom past the camera.)

TED: *(O S)* I've heard you can hire one of these guys and they'll show you around the city. For five bucks. They'll show you all the sights.

Scene 18

(MAX gathers the toys from the floor, untouched, and exits.)

(YEN, KOLAB, and LIDA stand staring out a window.)

(SISTER MARGARET enters with a mop and bucket, finds them staring.)

SISTER MARGARET: What are my little angels doing up here?

YEN: Kolab wanted to look.

LIDA: We wanted to see what was outside.

SISTER MARGARET: It's a street.

LIDA: Where are those kids going?

SISTER MARGARET: They're coming home from school.

LIDA: Oh.

KOLAB: Can we go?

SISTER MARGARET: We have a school here.

LIDA: Where?

SISTER MARGARET: In the room next door. We use two of the rooms up here as classrooms.

LIDA: I want to go to that school.

SISTER MARGARET: You haven't tried ours yet, have you.

YEN: Why can't we go to that one out there?

SISTER MARGARET: Because we have one in here.

YEN: It's not as good.

LIDA: Those kids have nicer clothes. And they all match.

SISTER MARGARET: Just because they wear uniforms doesn't mean it's better.

KOLAB: Can't we go out and meet them?

SISTER MARGARET: No. Not yet.

KOLAB: Please?

LIDA: They look like they're having fun.

SISTER MARGARET: So are you.

YEN: No were not. No one has fun here.

SISTER MARGARET: Of course we do. I'm fun.

(The girls stare at SISTER MARGARET.*)*

SISTER MARGARET: I am a fun person.

(The girls laugh.)

SISTER MARGARET: I am offended by that.

YEN: How old are you?

SISTER MARGARET: Two hundred and seven.

(The girls laugh.)

YEN: Nuh uh.

*(*KOLAB *can't keep her eyes off the street activity.)*

KOLAB: Look, she has a bicycle!

LIDA: So does she!

KOLAB: I want a bicycle.

LIDA: Me too.

KOLAB: Oh, look how many ! I want one!

(YEN *moves away from the window.*)

LIDA: I'd like to ride a bicycle. Have you ever ridden one, Yen?

YEN: Of course.

LIDA: I would ride it up and down the street. Up and down.

KOLAB: Me too. I want a red one.

LIDA: I want blue.

KOLAB: Can you buy us a bicycle lady?

SISTER MARGARET: No.

KOLAB: Why not?

SISTER MARGARET: What if all the girls here wanted bicycles?

KOLAB: We could share.

LIDA: Yes.

KOLAB: All the other kids get to ride bicycles and go to school.

LIDA: We want to do what they do.

YEN: We can't do what those kids do.

KOLAB: Why not?

YEN: We're bad.

SISTER MARGARET: Enough of that, Yen. There's nothing bad about you. You're all sweet, lovely girls and I want you all to wash up for dinner. I'll put fresh pajamas in the office for you to change into tonight, Okay? And a nice doctor is coming here in the morning. You will like her very much.

(YEN *rolls her eyes.*)

SISTER MARGARET: She always brings candy.

YEN: Always?

SISTER MARGARET: Everybody gets a piece of candy.

KOLAB: Does she bring bicycles?

SISTER MARGARET: No.

KOLAB: Oh.

SISTER MARGARET: Run along girls…I've got work to do.

(KOLAB *and* LIDA *remain transfixed by the window.*)

SISTER MARGARET: I said, run along please…

(*The three girls exit.*)

(SISTER MARGARET *stops working, and stares out the window herself.*)

Scene 19

(*Video:*)

(*The loud hum and blurry shot of driving at night from the back of a moto bike.*)

Scene 20

(*Bar*)

(SIDNEY *sits at a table overlooking the Mekong River. Beer in front of him. He stares at the view.*)

(JONATHON *enters with two beers.*)

JONATHON: Nice view.
(*Silence*)
If that river could talk, huh?
(*He helps himself to the seat beside* SIDNEY, *puts his beer in front of him.*)

SIDNEY: Next time check with me before you treat my shelter like an fucking orphanage.

JONATHON: They seem like nice people to me. Pictures of their house looked nice. Fresh sod lawn and lots of space to—

SIDNEY: One of these days, this part of the world will *not* be seen as a *hatchery* for sex traders and lonely Western couples with Chemlawns.

JONATHON: I didn't come here to argue—

SIDNEY: Someday a child in Southeast Asia might just get a fighting chance to stay with her own family.

JONATHON: I didn't come here to argue. Although, I don't see anything wrong with wanting a better life, a big back yard and a decent school district—

(SIDNEY *finally looks at* JONATHON.)

SIDNEY: What do you want?

JONATHON: Margaret told me I might find you here.

SIDNEY: Really?

JONATHON: After I promised to tell you to go home.

SIDNEY: I'm busy.

JONATHON: Listen…I know I made a few mistakes. But I think I could learn from you. If you'd allow me to pick your brain a bit—

SIDNEY: Not interested.

JONATHON: I'm humbling myself here.

SIDNEY: I'm sure that's painful for you.

JONATHON: C'mon…I know I fucked up. My boss in Washington called me this morning to tell me that I had personally humiliated the entire Action for All organization. And that my mistake, had also managed to embarrass our new biggest advocate and funder, the U S government.

SIDNEY: And?

JONATHON: If I want to stay on, I have to prove to him, immediately, that I'm capable of meeting the challenges of this job.

SIDNEY: Better start packing your bags.

JONATHON: I'm serious, Sidney. This is not good. The U S Government was going to use Action for All as it's new poster child for combating the sex trade… This is not good.

(JONATHON *and* SIDNEY *each take a sip of beer.* JONATHON *peels his shirt from his chest, tries to fan in some cool air.*)

JONATHON: Do you ever get used to this goddamn heat?

SIDNEY: You grew up in Texas.

JONATHON: We have air-conditioners. *(Silence)* You have a family here?

SIDNEY: Uh huh.

JONATHON: Kids?

SIDNEY: Yes.

JONATHON: How many?

SIDNEY: Two.

JONATHON: Really? Boys? Girls?

SIDNEY: One of each.

JONATHON: Were they born here?

SIDNEY: Yes.

JONATHON: Is your wife Cambodian?

SIDNEY: Vietnamese.

(Silence)

JONATHON: Where'd you meet her?

SIDNEY: In a bar.

JONATHON: Was she a waitress?

SIDNEY: She was a bar girl.

JONATHON: Really?

SIDNEY: Yes.

JONATHON: Interesting…

SIDNEY: Does that surprise you?

JONATHON: A little.

SIDNEY: You know what a bar girl is?

JONATHON: Of course.

(Silence)

Did it start off as, as a paid affair—I mean, did you—

SIDNEY: I was working for the U N. I hadn't been here long. I didn't know many people. I used to go out drinking by myself. We started talking at the bar.

JONATHON: Sure.

SIDNEY: She told me about her life. It was devastating. I was fascinated. She was strong and fragile and broken and beautiful…and…I fell in love.

JONATHON: Oh.

SIDNEY: It was never a paid affair.

JONATHON: You want another beer?

SIDNEY: I'm still working on this one, thanks.

(Silence. JONATHON finishes his beer.)

JONATHON: Can I ask you a really personal question?

SIDNEY: I thought you just did.

JONATHON: Why did you get into this field?

SIDNEY: I saw a need.

JONATHON: And?

SIDNEY: That's not enough?

JONATHON: How do you keep doing it?

SIDNEY: There's still a need.

JONATHON: I know…it's just…I've been thinking…
when I was training to come here and reading and
studying and riding on the plane over here…I just…I
felt like I wanted to ask someone who works in this
field…I could never get the courage to ask it in the
States…I guess I was waiting to come and see for
myself and now I see…and I wanted to ask someone
who works with these little girls everyday and—

SIDNEY: So ask it.

JONATHON: Do you think about what they've done?

SIDNEY: Done?

JONATHON: What do you do when you think about
what these girls have done?

SIDNEY: In the brothel?

JONATHON: Yes. I just…what do you do with those
thoughts…of the things they've had to do in there. To
men. What do you do with those thoughts of…of the
sex acts that these girls have had to perform? Do you
think about it?

SIDNEY: Of course.

JONATHON: Well, how do you stop thinking about it?

SIDNEY: I don't.

JONATHON: Does it make you feel guilty?

SIDNEY: I didn't perform those acts on the girls.

JONATHON: I know, but—

SIDNEY: And they didn't ask to be put in the position
they're in. They didn't choose to be trafficked. Stuck in
the sex trade. Stuck in a brothel.

JONATHON: I know—

SIDNEY: They're bodies aren't even built for the things they've had to do… Blow jobs that make them gag…sodomy and intercourse that rips them apart. Disfigures some of them. There's no guilt in thinking about it. It fuels my anger… There's nothing pretty or erotic or exciting in those images. I'd be a fucked up bastard to be in my position and find pleasure in those thoughts.

JONATHON: I'm not talking about pleasure.

SIDNEY: What are you talking about?

JONATHON: Sex, I guess.

SIDNEY: It's rape.

(Silence)

JONATHON: I guess I just don't know how to look at them as kids without thinking about the adult things they've done.

SIDNEY: Then maybe you're not cut out for this kind of work.

Scene 21

(YEN, KOLAB and LIDA stand as they did at the opening of the play, but in a corner, together this time.)

(TED enters this small area, and looks them over. He's still holding his video camera.)

YEN: No cameras.

(TED nods and quickly puts it away. He is still trying to decide which girl to choose.)

(He smiles awkwardly and the girls try and smile in return.)

(He points to LIDA. LIDA looks to YEN and KOLAB, before slowly walking off stage.)

(He begins to follow LIDA, *when he points to* YEN *as well. He wants both of them. He waits.)*

*(*YEN *exits in the same direction as* LIDA.*)*

*(*TED *follows.)*

*(*KOLAB *is left alone on stage, watching them leave her behind.)*

END OF ACT ONE

ACT TWO

Scene 22

(One week later)

(Morning. SIDNEY's office)

(SIDNEY is now the one sleeping in his office, the girls have moved in to the main sleeping quarters in the shelter.)

(SISTER MARGARET enters with coffee, waking him up.)

SISTER MARGARET: Rise and shine, you miserable man.

SIDNEY: Who says I'm miserable.

SISTER MARGARET: This is not good for you. Or your kids.

(SIDNEY sits up.)

SIDNEY: It might not come as any surprise, but I am enjoying this "vacation" from disappointing my family on a nightly basis.

SISTER MARGARET: Oh, you think you're free of that, do you?

SIDNEY: Yes.

SISTER MARGARET: No.

SIDNEY: It's possible.

SISTER MARGARET: No.

SIDNEY: How do you know?

SISTER MARGARET: Your kids are waiting for you to come home. They're waiting for you to make up to their mother and come home with toys and diamonds and I'm sorry presents and make it all better.

SIDNEY: Butt out.

SISTER MARGARET: It's true.

SIDNEY: For someone who's never been married and never had kids, you seem to think you know a lot.

SISTER MARGARET: It's the wisdom of observation.

SIDNEY: Sure.

SISTER MARGARET: You need—

SIDNEY: To drink my coffee in peace. Without your advice. But thank you.

(SISTER MARGARET *notices some new drawings on the wall.*)

SISTER MARGARET: Did our little Kolab draw this?

SIDNEY: Yes.

SISTER MARGARET: Sweet, huh?

SIDNEY: I think she's adjusting pretty well.

SISTER MARGARET: She's making friends. Speaking up. Lida's more secure. They're both very popular with the rest of the girls.

SIDNEY: And Yen?

SISTER MARGARET: God bless her…. But I'll break through. Give me time…. She's all thorns on the outside, mush and starved for love on the inside.

(SISTER MARGARET *continues looking at the new drawings, while* SIDNEY *stays focused on his coffee.*)

SISTER MARGARET: So many new pictures, Sidney. Max is keeping them busy… Look at the way Lida's drawn this man's hands. They look like hooks, eh?

SIDNEY: Yeah.

SISTER MARGARET: And his nose looks like a carrot…
(Upon closer inspection)
…He looks like a snowman.

SIDNEY: I wonder if that was the first white man she met.

SISTER MARGARET: First white man, but Max said she had been in the brothel for awhile…she met her share of Cambodian men as well.

SIDNEY: She didn't draw any pictures of them.

SISTER MARGARET: I see that.

SIDNEY: The white bastard left an impression.

(SISTER MARGARET takes a seat with the weight of her thoughts.)

SISTER MARGARET: *(Sighs)* These little angels' first impression of the Western world is a sweaty snowman shoving his penis down their throats for thirty dollars…up their bum for forty dollars…and they know their options are gone, they're soiled women now…and if they were a so-called "untarnished" woman, with the only other job for women *outside* the brothel in this country, they'd be working in a factory for the same amount of money, forty dollars for a month's work, sewing T-shirts for Eddie Bauer and the Gap and Marks and Spencer, for all I know… Either way, some white bastard is taking the best years of their lives.
(Sighs)
Where's God in that?

SIDNEY: You're the Catholic.

(SIDNEY puts on his shoes. He's touched a nerve in SISTER MARGARET. He can feel her silence.)

SIDNEY: What?

SISTER MARGARET: Just once I'd like to have a
philosophical discussion about something—

SIDNEY: Sounds theological to me—

SISTER MARGARET: Without you using the same old
"You're the Catholic" response. It's so damn irritating,
Sidney. Every time. "You're the Catholic, Margaret".
For heavens sake. Because I'm a Catholic doesn't mean
I don't have doubts and questions about the tragic
nature of life. I've seen too much of this world not to
have questions. To ponder justice. You insult my years
of experience and my intelligence when you—

SIDNEY: I'm sorry.

SISTER MARGARET: I'm a far more complicated person
than you ever give me credit for.

SIDNEY: I know. I'm sorry—

SISTER MARGARET: Sometimes I think that you assume,
because I took a vow of chastity as a young woman,
that I can't "really" comprehend what these girls have
gone through.

SIDNEY: I've never said that.

SISTER MARGARET: Oh, you didn't need to. It's in your
arrogance.

SIDNEY: My arrogance?

SISTER MARGARET: You patronize me sometimes,
Sidney.

SIDNEY: How?

SISTER MARGARET: You think a woman has to have had
sex with a man to understand the trauma these little
girls have experienced.

SIDNEY: That's not true.

SISTER MARGARET: No?

SIDNEY: No. But, yes…okay…maybe…in some ways…I see your life as a bit of a…sheltered one.

SISTER MARGARET: See.

SIDNEY: And to believe in a Pope and church with so much corruption, abuse, that doesn't believe in birth control.

SISTER MARGARET: Who spent four years of her life in Africa passing out condoms?

SIDNEY: I know you did, but—

SISTER MARGARET: And four more years taking care of AIDS victims—if you think that I don't believe in—

SIDNEY: But you've never left the church.

SISTER MARGARET: You think that's a contradiction on my part?

SIDNEY: Yes.

SISTER MARGARET: Cambodia is a country full of corruption and contradictions, Sidney, and you haven't left it.

SIDNEY: No, but I have family here now.

SISTER MARGARET: That's working out very well at the moment.

SIDNEY: Okay, okay.

SISTER MARGARET: The church is my family.

SIDNEY: I don't know where this conversation is going, but you obviously woke up with a bee in your bonnet—

SISTER MARGARET: My point, Sidney, is that a person can have contradictions in her character and country and beliefs and still do the good work in the world she feels called to do.

SIDNEY: I don't disagree with that—

SISTER MARGARET: And the reasons a person is called to help these little angels…may have nothing to do with being a Catholic…the reasons may be just as complicated and confusing…and private…as the woman herself.

(Silence)

SIDNEY: I suppose so.

SISTER MARGARET: If you'll excuse me, I've got my little darlings to wake.
(She begins to exit.)

SIDNEY: I'm sorry, Margaret. I don't know what kind of God lets people suffer the way they do.

(Silence)

SISTER MARGARET: That's why we're a good team, Mr. Webb. I know you aren't waiting around for answers. You simply plunge forward. Get things done.

SIDNEY: Thanks.

SISTER MARGARET: While I believe that all of those things you do, and do well, and that I am here to help you with, are the actions of God.

(SIDNEY puts his hands together and bows his head in the gesture [Sompiah] that is the Cambodian and Buddhist greeting and gesture of thanks.)

(SISTER MARGARET puts her hands together and bows in return.)

SISTER MARGARET: Now get dressed.
(She exits.)

(SIDNEY smiles and continues getting dressed.)

Scene 23

(TED *hides as he surrounded by the screams of young girls, caught in the middle of the raid of the brothel. He is frantically zipping up his pants, buckling his belt.*)

(*He disappears in the dark.*)

Scene 24

(*The shelter courtyard*)

(YEN *enters the stage alone.*)

(*She finds a doll and a book on the ground. She picks up the doll first and examines it like a foreign object. Looks under the dress. Touches the eyes on the face. Touches the hands. Turns it around to see the back of it, then back to the front. Looks at the face*)

(*Awkwardly, she holds it close to her, for just one second, closer. To test what that might feel like—*)

(*The sound of other girls laughing and talking float around her.*)

(*She throws the doll aside and picks up the book. She sits down and looks at the doll. Then begins to swing her legs in a chair, and thumb through the book.*)

(SIDNEY *enters.* YEN *looks at him then returns to her book.*)

SIDNEY: Beautiful day, huh?

(YEN *turns the page.* SIDNEY *moves closer.*)

SIDNEY: What are you reading?

(YEN *shows* SIDNEY *the book.*)

SIDNEY: You like to read? We have a pretty good library—

YEN: I don't know how to read.

SIDNEY: I see. Well, what have you been learning in class?

YEN: How to sit still.
(She returns to turning the pages.)

SIDNEY: That's a good skill… One I've never quite mastered. What about you?

YEN: What?

SIDNEY: Are you good at it?

YEN: No.

SIDNEY: I guess we have something in common.
(YEN shrugs, keeps her eyes on the book.)

SIDNEY: Max tells me you have a birthday coming up.

YEN: I thought Max was supposed to keep things a secret.

SIDNEY: Is your birthday a secret?

YEN: No.

SIDNEY: Then he didn't do anything wrong.
(YEN shrugs.)

SIDNEY: Well…he did tell me one other thing.

YEN: What?

SIDNEY: That you're not happy here.

YEN: That's not a secret.

SIDNEY: I guess not.
(Silence)
Why do you think you're not happy?
(YEN shrugs.)

SIDNEY: You miss your friends?

YEN: Yes.

SIDNEY: I can understand that.

(He takes a seat.)
I have a lot of friends I wish I could see. That live a
long way from here. I have some friends I haven't seen
in fifteen years.

YEN: But you could see them, if you wanted to.

SIDNEY: It would take a lot of effort—

YEN: No one will let me see my friends now.

(Silence)

SIDNEY: You want to go back?

YEN: Yes.

SIDNEY: Why?

YEN: Because people like me there.

SIDNEY: People like you here.

YEN: No they don't.

SIDNEY: Have you given them a chance?

(YEN looks around the stage. SIDNEY follows her eyes.)

YEN: All these girls think they will have a better life,
but doing what? Sewing shirts in a factory? Selling
shampoo and cigarettes on the sidewalk? Cutting hair
in a beauty shop?

SIDNEY: What's wrong with that?

YEN: It's stupid.

SIDNEY: Why?

YEN: No one wants us.

SIDNEY: That's not true—

YEN: No one will ever love us. Or marry us.

SIDNEY: Why?

YEN: We're dirty.

SIDNEY: That's not true—

YEN: Boys are like gold, girls are like cotton.

SIDNEY: I know, I know—

YEN: Gold will always be gold, but once cotton is dirty, it's worthless.

SIDNEY: I know that saying. It's a lie—

YEN: We have the same saying in Vietnam.

SIDNEY: Because it is said, doesn't mean you have to believe it.

YEN: What difference does it make? Everyone else does.

SIDNEY: I don't.

YEN: You can tell us what you want, Mr Webb, what you think is right, what you believe, what people believe in America, what Sister Margaret believes…but all these girls here, no matter how many times you tell us, no matter what you tell us, we all know inside, we *know*, who we are, what we are. That we are dirty, and can't ever be cleaned.

SIDNEY: I don't believe that.

(YEN *gestures around the shelter courtyard.*)

YEN: All this is just make-believe. A vacation. We will never really have all the things you try and tell us we will. We just pretend and let you enjoy watching us pretend.

(*Silence*)

SIDNEY: You're pretty smart for thirteen.

(*Silence*)

YEN: I may be fourteen. No one really remembers my birthday.

(SIDNEY *smiles.*)

YEN: I just made up that date from what a friend of my mother's told me once.

SIDNEY: I see.

YEN: I could be turning fifteen.

SIDNEY: Fifteen?

(YEN *shrugs*.)

SIDNEY: My wife was fifteen when she came here. From Vietnam.

YEN: Really?

SIDNEY: Uh huh.

YEN: I've heard she's pretty.

SIDNEY: She is.

YEN: Then why are you sleeping here?

SIDNEY: My wife was brought here just like you...she didn't ask to come...and like you, was working in a brothel, where she had many friends...they were her family...even after she started working in a bar, where I met her.

YEN: You met her in a bar?

SIDNEY: Yes. And I fell in love with her. And married her—

YEN: You love her?

SIDNEY: Yes—

YEN: Then why are you staying here?

SIDNEY: It's complicated. My point is, for years she thought she was dirty...even after we were married, she would still cry sometimes because she was convinced I would leave her—

YEN: You did leave her.

SIDNEY: No. I didn't. I didn't leave her because of that…I haven't left her…I just…I would never leave her because of that, Yen. Ever. And any man who would is dirt, not gold. You understand?

YEN: I can't count on meeting a white man in a bar. I can't count on anything…I can't even count how old I really am.

(Silence)

Besides…the doctor says I'm sick. What does any of it matter anyway.

(SIDNEY wants to touch YEN's foot, give some comfort, but isn't sure how…he settles on touching the leg of her chair.)

(YEN quickly exits, passing TAM WEBB, SIDNEY's wife, as she enters. They share a glance. YEN gives a final glance back to SIDNEY before she exits for good.)

(TAM carries a bag. She's stunning.)

TAM: Is this what you do here all day?

SIDNEY: What?

TAM: Sit under trees. Laze around like a cat.

SIDNEY: No. Not usually—

TAM: It doesn't look so difficult to do. So…what do you call it…"challenging"?—

SIDNEY: Are the kids with you?

TAM: They're in school.

(Silence)

I thought you might like a change of clothes.

SIDNEY: Thanks.

TAM: That shirt could use an iron, you know.

SIDNEY: Probably.

TAM: Do you want me to take it with me? I can bring it back—

SIDNEY: No.

TAM: Okay. Fine. Everyone will think I'm lazy.
(Silence)
You look thin.

SIDNEY: I'm fine.

TAM: Margaret doesn't feed you enough?

SIDNEY: I'm fine, Tam.

TAM: You look terrible…I should have brought food.

SIDNEY: We have food here.

TAM: Okay. You don't need my food.
(Silence)
Where is everyone?

SIDNEY: It's just a calm in the storm, I think.

TAM: That's too bad.

SIDNEY: Why?

TAM: You like the storm.

SIDNEY: No I don't.

TAM: It makes you feel important.

(SIDNEY is holding his tongue.)

TAM: Saving the girls.

(SIDNEY sighs, trying to keep from arguing.)

SIDNEY: Thank you for the clothes, Tam. I appreciate it.
You didn't need to make the trip…but thank you.

(Silence, as neither SIDNEY nor TAM sure how to proceed.)

TAM: You look tired.

SIDNEY: I am.

TAM: Then come home.
(Silence)

Okay. Okay. I know. You don't want to talk to me. I
understand.

SIDNEY: Tam…

TAM: You like me better quiet.

SIDNEY: No.

TAM: Quiet and obedient.

SIDNEY: That's not true—

TAM: Full of gratitude. To my American husband.
Thank you, Mr Webb—

SIDNEY: Go home, Tam. I can't talk to you when you're
like this.

TAM: How?

SIDNEY: Tam—

TAM: How am I, Sidney?

SIDNEY: I've got work to do.

TAM: Am I boring to you now?

SIDNEY: No.

TAM: Do you hate me?

SIDNEY: No.

TAM: Then why won't you talk to me?

SIDNEY: Tam—

TAM: Why won't you touch me anymore? You think
I'm ugly and stupid—

SIDNEY: I can't talk to you when you're not rational,
Tam. It's impossible.

TAM: Okay. You want a smart, white, rational wife.
That's what you want now.

SIDNEY: No.

TAM: You're done with me...you want an easy, white woman who has a college education...who will never ask you to sleep with her at night.

SIDNEY: That's not true.

TAM: You want someone who understands things you don't think I understand...an intellectual lady ... who comes from a good family...a smart American woman who is rational all the time...a college girl from Connecticut just like you.

SIDNEY: No! Stop! God! See? ...Go home, Tam. Okay? Just go home and we can talk later...I've got work to do.

TAM: We won't talk later.

SIDNEY: Tam—

TAM: We never talk.

SIDNEY: Tam, please—

TAM: I cook, you eat, you play with the children, you go to sleep, you go to work—

SIDNEY: You wanted to separate.

TAM: I want a husband.

SIDNEY: I can't keep going in the same goddamn circles with you. It's exhausting.

TAM: That's what married people do.

SIDNEY: Not like us.

TAM: How do you know?

SIDNEY: It's different.

TAM: Because I am uneducated, Sidney?

SIDNEY: No—

TAM: Because I come from nothing?

SIDNEY: No—

TAM: Okay, I know. Because I am stupid and exhausting and scared...and I don't understand some of the college words you use...okay, that is who I am... okay. I know who I am, Sidney.... But I am still your wife. The only thing I am asking you to do is come home and talk to me... Talk to me like you love me. Maybe try and touch me. Even when I'm not rational.

SIDNEY: I've tried.

TAM: Try again.

SIDNEY: Why?

TAM: How awful it is to stand here. Begging. How pathetic I must seem to you—

SIDNEY: Why, Tam? ...So I can tell you the same things, over and over again? ...Things you refuse to believe? ...So I can tell the kids to go back to bed, don't worry, Mommy's okay...Daddy's not hurting her...Mommy's just sad... Why?

TAM: Because you love me.
(*She puts the bag beside* SIDNEY.)

TAM: Don't you?

SIDNEY: Yes.

TAM: Do you?

SIDNEY: Yes—

TAM: Do you still think I'm beautiful?

SIDNEY: Yes, Tam. I love you. Yes. I think you're very beautiful. It has nothing to do with that.

TAM: What does it have to do with?
(*Silence*)
Tell me.
(*Silence*)

TAM: Don't make me stand here. Lonely. I'm trying—
I'm rational right now, aren't I?

SIDNEY: You cry every time I touch you.

(Silence)

TAM: Not every time.

SIDNEY: I can't take it anymore.

TAM: I'm sorry.

SIDNEY: Don't apologize, Tam. (Shit.) Please. Please
don't apologize.

(Silence)

TAM: Okay then. Okay. I understand. I am quiet now.
I'll let you get back to work.

(Silence)

I know how important your work is to you.

(Silence)

Okay.

(She exits.)

Scene 25

*(TED sitting on his bed. Staring at the camera. His hair is
wet from a shower. He's holding the remote for the T V, as
the sound of the T V plays in the background.)*

TED: I'm having a great time here in Cambodia. Whew.
Wonderful. Mind-expanding. People are friendly. Food
is great... Uh, Everything's cheap. Yeah, it's really been
a top-notch trip. So far... Really been something. I've
seen a lot of great sights.

(He changes the channel.)

Really enjoying the sights.

Scene 26

(MAX *sits with* KOLAB *and* LIDA *and paper and crayons.*)

(KOLAB *takes a black crayon and just covers the entire paper with it.*)

(LIDA *spends the time deciding which crayons to use.*)

MAX: What are you drawing Kolab?

(He waits.)

Kolab? What are you drawing?

KOLAB: My mother.

MAX: We have other colors, if you want—

KOLAB: I know.

MAX: Why does she look like this?

KOLAB: I don't know.

MAX: Are you sure?

KOLAB: I like this color.

MAX: I see.

(KOLAB *keeps covering the paper with black crayon.*)

MAX: And Lida.

LIDA: What?

MAX: You haven't drawn anything.

LIDA: There is nothing to draw.

MAX: Nothing?

LIDA: No.

MAX: Nothing you're thinking about your family today?

(Silence)

LIDA: Can I sit in your lap, Mr Max?

MAX: No. I'm sorry. You can't.

LIDA: If you want me to, I will. I don't mind—

MAX: I don't want you to, Lida.

LIDA: Don't you like me?

MAX: Of course I like you…. But I will never ask you to do those kinds of things. I can like you, just because you're Lida…I've told you that. Right?

LIDA: Yes.

MAX: You don't have to do those things anymore.

LIDA: What if I just wanted to sit there?

(Silence)

MAX: I'm sorry.
(Silence)
I'm sorry, Lida… Do you want to talk about it?

(Silence)

LIDA: Do I have to talk today?

MAX: No. I guess not—

LIDA: Good.

(LIDA hands back the paper and crayons, and exits the stage. MAX watches her go as KOLAB stands up, hands her paper to MAX, and runs after LIDA.)

(MAX takes a moment for himself, then gathers the paper and crayons.)

Scene 27

(JONATHON finds SIDNEY still sitting alone in one of the two chairs. He gives the prayer and bow gesture of sompiah to SIDNEY.)

JONATHON: Mr Webb. Look at me. A regular native.

(SIDNEY stands and returns the gesture.)

SIDNEY: Great.

JONATHON: I like this custom. Really grows on you, huh?

SIDNEY: Uh huh.

JONATHON: Are you alright?

SIDNEY: I'm fine. I called your office and they said you were in Bangkok—

JONATHON: I was. I'm back now.
(Silence)
Say, uh, what happened to those little twins, those babies? That couple I met at the hotel that wanted to adopt them left me four messages that they are still looking—

SIDNEY: We found a relative of the mother who wanted to adopt them.

JONATHON: Oh.

SIDNEY: How was Bangkok?

JONATHON: But they could have had a big back yard. Their own rooms—

SIDNEY: There on business?

JONATHON: Where?

SIDNEY: Bangkok.

JONATHON: Oh. Yeah. Action for All had a conference.

SIDNEY: How'd it go?

JONATHON: Four days of long boring meetings about the continued increase in the sex trade and sex trafficking, new international anti-trafficking laws and the details of those laws, who wrote them and why, and to conclude, power point lectures on the growing impossibilities of stopping sex trafficking in Southeast Asia.

SIDNEY: Productive.

JONATHON: "The sex trade is to Southeast Asia what oil is to Saudi Arabia and Iraq."

SIDNEY: Was that the slogan of the week?

JONATHON: "It's just a different kind of war."
(He inhales and exhales a deep breath.)
By the end of it, I had to stop listening.
(Whispers)
Tried a little "recreational" drugs to just to get my head back on straight. Whew… It's everywhere there.

SIDNEY: Uh huh.

JONATHON: Those little trips to my subconscious could get habit forming.

SIDNEY: Did you find anything?

JONATHON: Where?
(He finally gets the joke, but doesn't laugh.)
Oh.

SIDNEY: You visiting the shelter for any particular reason today?

JONATHON: No. Just checking in…I wanted to see how my "small victories in the midst of my big failure" are doing.

SIDNEY: Uh. Well, the two youngest are doing great, actually.

JONATHON: Really?

SIDNEY: They are getting counseling and are sleeping better and making friends… They've become obsessed with getting and riding bicycles, but we don't really have the money or the room.

JONATHON: Really. Now that makes me feel happy. I'm glad to hear that, Mr Webb. I really am.
(He takes a seat in YEN's chair.)

To tell you the truth, that goddamn conference got me
so depressed…Jesus…I thought "what the hell was
I thinking? …Human Rights? …I could be making
some real money in Houston defending housewives in
divorce court? …I could be raking it in just shuffling
papers in patent law!"

SIDNEY: That would be satisfying.

JONATHON: The drug trade would be downright
refreshing after this, I swear…and I like the pot over
here…and that hashish I had in Bankok…I could
get used to that… Which kind of disturbs me…I see
how folks can get hooked on the stuff. It feels good…
Everything's fine when you're high…and it really
helps ease the pain when your boss is tearing you a
new one… This next raid has to go off without a hitch.

SIDNEY: Next raid?

JONATHON: Yeah. I've been busy trying to organize our
next raid.

SIDNEY: Uh huh.

JONATHON: Please don't give me that look…. We're
going to work with the police this time.
(He takes a cell phone from his pocket, and shows it to
SIDNEY.)
I've got a direct line…I'll let everyone know what's
going on. I'm doing it by the books. Whatever the hell
that means here. But I can't get one goddamn person
to return my call. I think the police are laughing
behind my back…I do… Turds… And I've already got
people asking for money and favors…What a fucking
headache…

SIDNEY: When is this next raid going to happen?

JONATHON: Oh, I don't know yet. Rest assured. I'll keep
you informed this time.
(Silence)

You'd probably be interested to know, that my boss
told me, as he was tearing me a new
asshole..."but giving me a chance to prove him
wrong"...that he's not sure I'm cut out
for this kind of work.
(He takes in the courtyard.)
Hell. My father told me point blank I wasn't as he was
dropping me off at the airport.
(Using a thick Texas accent)
"Son, why do you have to go across the goddamn
ocean to prove that you want to help the needy
and change the world. America has poor people
and prostitutes, don't we? ...Have you been to Las
Vegas? ....You can help them, can't you? ...You just
don't have the personality of those folks working for
Oxfam and Unicef and so forth, son. They're scrappy.
They're tough. Doctors, not lawyers. They're skinny
vegetarians who don't mind a bug bite or two while
they're picking snot out of some starving babies nose
or shoveling shit from a john...You don't even like
your, your shoes to get scuffed, son. You're uptight.
Got a B+ on your report card once and cried for a
month...You're afraid of failure...You hate change.
You're impatient ...Your house looks like a goddamn
ad from your Mother's *Good Housekeeping* magazine.
Dirt and women and kids make you nervous. If I didn't
know you better, I might think you're a fairy..."

SIDNEY: Nice.

JONATHON: He's waiting at the airport, right now, with
a big sign, in block letters, "Welcome home, son. I told
you so."

SIDNEY: He would get along with my Dad.

JONATHON: Your Dad give you a hard time?

SIDNEY: Leaving the States was the only thing that ever
made our relationship possible.

JONATHON: Yeah?

SIDNEY: He wanted other things for me.

JONATHON: Like what?

SIDNEY: Security. Sacrifice. A forty-year mortgage. All the things he hated about his own life.

JONATHON: So what'd you do?

SIDNEY: Stayed. Here.

(KOLAB *and* LIDA *enter kicking a ball.*)

(JONATHON *stops it and kicks it back to* KOLAB.)

KOLAB: Thank you.

(KOLAB *kicks the ball to* LIDA *and they exit the stage as* JONATHON *and* SIDNEY *watch.*)

JONATHON: What do you think their fathers wanted for them?

SIDNEY: I don't know… Food.

JONATHON: Why didn't you give those babies a chance to go to the States? I just don't get it.

SIDNEY: It would have been illegal. A little thing called human trafficking.

JONATHON: You might have found a loop hole…I mean, c'mon, look around you…you of all people knows how difficult this country is for little girls, for women.

SIDNEY: This is their home.

JONATHON: Still.

SIDNEY: Why do you think I stayed in Cambodia?

JONATHON: You like the beer girls.

(SIDNEY *doesn't respond.*)

JONATHON: I'm sorry.

SIDNEY: Have you noticed anything since you've been here?

JONATHON: Well—

SIDNEY: You are in an incredible place...with yes, it's lion share of damage and corruption and problems and poverty...and yet, yet look how wonderful the people are...look how people smile and bow and pray and laugh...despite so much destruction and trauma... despite murder and betrayal by each other...look how people have carried on and continue to persevere in this country...there's a kind of courage and patience and beauty here, that I don't think I ever felt at home.... Or I never took the time to feel it. Maybe that's the difference.

(The sound of girls laughing O S)

JONATHON: But if you could have given one of them a chance to get out of here, to go live with a family in the United States, live in a nice house, get an education, you wouldn't do it?

(Silence)

SIDNEY: No.

JONATHON: Why not?

SIDNEY: Botox, breast implants, bulimia, Britney Spears, and everything else that begins with B and ends with teenage girls roaming the mall—

JONATHON: That's ridiculous and selfish. Those are choices—

SIDNEY: Or expectations.

JONATHON: *Choices.* Please. At least they have choices. C'mon, Sidney. It's a safer place—

SIDNEY: For shopping for clothes they don't need?

JONATHON: To live. To grow up.

SIDNEY: I don't think that's the answer to the problem.
I've got work to do—

JONATHON: What's the answer?

(SIDNEY *searches…the impossible answer. Gestures toward*
JONATHON)

SIDNEY: Action for All?

(*The sound of the all the girls in the courtyard surround
them, growing louder.*)

(SIDNEY *exits.*)

(JONATHON *is left alone on stage.*)

(YEN *enters.*)

(YEN *stares at him as she walks across the stage. She walks
very close to him, but does not touch him.*)

(JONATHON *tries to smile.*)

JONATHON: Hi Yen.

(YEN *stays close.* JONATHON *isn't sure what to do.*)

(YEN *just stares at him.* JONATHON *tries to smile.*)

(*The sexual tension is palpable.*)

(YEN *pulls a hidden cigarette from her dress, and a lighter.
She lights the cigarette.*)

(JONATHON *takes the cigarette from her mouth.*)

(YEN *keeps walking.*)

(JONATHON *watches as she exits.*)

Scene 28

(TED *in his hotel, eyes red. Hair and face wet from another
shower. Trying to smile. T V playing in the background*)

TED: Very hot here. Very dirty. Three showers. And
counting.

Scene 29

(The sound of the courtyard full of girls voices fade on
KOLAB *and* LIDA *staring out the window, the ball at their
feet. They're waiting for something outside.)*

KOLAB: Where are they?

LIDA: I don't know.

KOLAB: Maybe there's no school today.

LIDA: Maybe.

*(*KOLAB *and* LIDA *wait.)*

KOLAB: Here they come.

LIDA: There they are.

KOLAB: There's the tall one.

LIDA: Look at her hair. She's wearing pigtails.

KOLAB: She's got new ribbons.

LIDA: Blue.

KOLAB: Lucky.

LIDA: There's the fat one. She's got candy in her hand. I
can see it.

KOLAB: Yen likes that kind of candy.

LIDA: I like it too.

*(*KOLAB *and* LIDA *both stand watching.)*

KOLAB: Do you miss her?

LIDA: Who?

KOLAB: Mamma.

LIDA: No.

KOLAB: I do.

LIDA: Hey look, there's the boy with the blue bicycle—

KOLAB: Sometimes she was nice.

LIDA: Maybe.

KOLAB: With the candy. She was nice—

LIDA: Look, he's leaving. And the girl is riding with him.

KOLAB: Maybe that's his sister.

LIDA: She's so pretty and tall.

(KOLAB *and* LIDA *watch.*)

LIDA: I wish I could be his sister.

KOLAB: He'd let you ride on his bicycle if you were his sister.

LIDA: And maybe he could tell our parents to buy me a bicycle. For my birthday. Tell them to buy the same color. Exactly the same. Just like his.

KOLAB: No, tell him to ask for red.

LIDA: No.

KOLAB: Red for you.

LIDA: No. We'd both have *blue* bicycles, riding down the street from school in our clean uniforms. Riding riding riding…happy happy…la la la…

(KOLAB *laughs.*)

KOLAB: La…la…la…

(YEN *enters and watches the girls from the corner of the stage.*)

LIDA: Happy happy happy…And we'd get home to our parents….la la la…"Hi mother, Hi father…guess what we learned in school today? …"What children? What did you learn?"…Nothing! But we've got these great bicycles and we got ribbons and we got you and so we don't care what we learn as long as we can ride wherever we want…we're happy when we're riding— riding…

KOLAB: Riding riding—

LIDA: Riding all around the city as fast as we can because we can ride and see the chickens in the market and we can see the fancy clothes in the stores and we can ride to the river and watch the boats on the river go up and down up and down and the people waving from the boats and we wave back "hello people out there on your boats!"..."hello people out there on your boats!"

KOLAB: "Hello…"

LIDA: "What's it like out there on the water?"

KOLAB: "It's warm and misty!"

LIDA: Misty?

KOLAB: Yeah.

LIDA: "What are you catching out there?"

KOLAB: "Nothing."

LIDA: "Nothing? Why aren't you catching fish?"

KOLAB: "We're not here to catch fish. We're just sailing by."

LIDA: "Where are you going?"

KOLAB: "We don't know. We're just floating with the river. Floating with the breeze."

LIDA: "Floating with the breeze? With the river? What if it takes you somewhere you don't want to go?"

KOLAB: "What?"

LIDA: "What if the river takes you somewhere you don't want to go?"

KOLAB: "I can't hear you! The mist is in my ears!"

LIDA: "What if it takes you away…"

KOLAB: "I can't hear you, but I sure like your bicycles! You're lucky to have the nice new bicycles, but I really think you should have asked for red!"

LIDA: I don't want red.

KOLAB: "Everyone knows red is better, little girl"

LIDA: Why?

KOLAB: "Red is the color of the sun, and you can always tell where you are from the sun!"

LIDA: "Not if don't know where you are and you don't know where you're going."

KOLAB: "Good-bye little girl...good-bye little boy...our boat is moving faster...the river is taking us away... into the sun...who knows where we'll be tomorrow..."

LIDA: "Good-bye."

KOLAB: "Good luck to you and your happy happy family...la...la...la."

LIDA: And we'd watch the boat keep floating down the river and we wouldn't stop waving until we couldn't see anymore of their hands waving back at us...their hands are too small to see...their hands are gone on the river...their boat is gone...we don't know where they're going...but we'd ride home to our parents and say hello mother and father we're so glad our house is on land and what's for dinner?

KOLAB: I hope it's duck.

LIDA: Happy happy happy...

YEN: La...la...la...

(KOLAB *and* LIDA *stop.*)

YEN: Everyone's been looking for you.

KOLAB: We, we were just playing—

LIDA: A silly game—

YEN: Hurry up. Dinner's ready. Everyone's waiting.

(KOLAB *and* LIDA *exit.*)

(YEN *stands in front of the window, looking outside.*)

(*She walks through it, into the dark, The stage is empty.*)

Scene 30

(SIDNEY *and* SISTER MARGARET *enter slowly, looking through the same window.* JONATHON *follows.*)

JONATHON: How'd she get out?

(*No one answers him.*)

(MAX *enters.*)

(*They survey the window/stage.*)

JONATHON: Huh? How the hell did she get out?

MAX: How's it look like she got out?

JONATHON: Well, Jesus… Why don't you have bars up here—you should have bars on these windows.

SISTER MARGARET: No—

JONATHON: Of course you should. Look what happens. You need bars on these windows.

MAX: No.

JONATHON: Yes.

SISTER MARGARET: You can't make these little angels live in another cage. I won't have it.

JONATHON: That's ridiculous.

MAX: Why?

JONATHON: They can escape any time they want.

MAX: So it's better to remind them they can't?

JONATHON: Yes… See… She must have climbed across that rooftop and down. I bet she had someone to meet her…Jesus.

(No one answers JONATHON.*)*

JONATHON: Well, I'm going to look for her. I can't just stand around—

SIDNEY: No…

JONATHON: What do you mean, no? I'll go get her and bring her back.

MAX: We can't make her stay here.

JONATHON: Yes we can. I'm calling the police.

MAX: They won't do anything—

JONATHON: What?

MAX: If she wants to go. We can't force her—

JONATHON: She's thirteen!

(No one answers JONATHON.*)*

JONATHON: Sidney?

*(*SIDNEY *doesn't look at* JONATHON.*)*

JONATHON: *This* is your answer to the problem?

(No one answers JONATHON.*)*

JONATHON: What's the matter with you people?

(No one answers JONATHON.*)*

*(*JONATHON *exits, reaching for his cell phone.)*

SIDNEY: *(Quietly)* Goddamn it.
(He slowly exits.)

SISTER MARGARET: God bless her….

*(*MAX *and* SISTER MARGARET *remain staring out the window.)*

SISTER MARGARET: The little ones will be crushed.

Max: Yes.

Scene 31

(The river)

(JONATHON enters, out of breath. He's exhausted and angry. He looks around, one last time.)

(He dials his cell phone. No answer. [Again] He slaps it shut.)

(He puts the phone in his pocket, and finds a joint.)

(He lights the joint, and inhales, shaking his head at yet another "failure".)

(He tries to let the pot take effect.)

(He sits down. He takes his cell phone from his pocket, and slides it away from him. Fuck it.)

(Defeated, he puts his head in his hands.)

(On the other side of the stage, TED enters with his luggage and camera, his camera pointed at the river.)

(Video/same time: Shot of the river as small boats float by. People standing in them, easing there way with the water.)

TED: Ted Thompson. Was here.

(TED stands there filming.)

(He brings the camera down.)

(JONATHON keeps his head in his hands, smoking.)

Scene 32

(The shelter)

(KOLAB and LIDA stand at the window. Staring out. Waiting for YEN to return.)

(They remain staring during the next scene.)

Scene 33

(Night)

(The river)

(YEN prays to the river.)

YEN: Hello Mekong…I am Yen…I came from Vietnam a little girl. I come back to you an old woman. I am asking you take me with you tonight. Please. Take me down your river to Vietnam and leave my on the shores of my homeland… Please… That is all I ask of you…I don't care how long it takes. I don't care how you get me there…I don't care who finds me. I don't care if no one knows who I am and I am ugly and awful. I don't care if fish feed on my body and boats don't stop to take me on board. I don't care if all my bones scatter and nothing but my hands reach the edge of Vietnam…but let these fingers grab the soil where I was born one last time so that this girl may end and someone new begin…. Just take me home where I belong so that I can start again. Start fresh. Safe and new. Give me new courage. Give me new eyes. Give me new parents… Bring me back in a warm home. Bring me back in a new body. Healthy and free… Bring me back, as a boy. *(She walks into the river.)*

Scene 34

(Morning)

(SIDNEY reads the Cambodia Daily *and* SISTER MARGARET *sits beside him. Both are drinking their morning coffee.)*

SIDNEY: ""Action for All" has decided to pull out its operations in Cambodia after a brief effort at combating the child sex trade in Phnom Penh. Upon receiving dozens of threats from unknown parties, which they believe are connected to the Cambodian military and police, the organization concluded, "this country is not an environment conducive to our long-term plans..."

(SISTER MARGARETt gestures for SIDNEY to hand the paper to her. He passes the paper. She glances at the article, and puts the paper down.)

SISTER MARGARET: No surprises there.

SIDNEY: No. I guess not.

(Silence. He moves the blanket and pillow aside from where he's been sleeping.)

SISTER MARGARET: I've called your wife. She's coming to get you.

SIDNEY: Why?

SISTER MARGARET: I'm sick of you.

SIDNEY: Margaret—

SISTER MARGARET: You're getting too comfortable sleeping here.

SIDNEY: Who says I'm comfortable.

SISTER MARGARET: This place is not going to fall apart with out you.

SIDNEY: I've never said it would—

SISTER MARGARET: You have your own children who need you.

SIDNEY: Margaret please—

SISTER MARGARET: And you're unhappy.

SIDNEY: I'm not.

SISTER MARGARET: Please. Look at yourself.

SIDNEY: I think I look fine. Handsome even.

SISTER MARGARET: Please.

SIDNEY: I like my job, Margaret. I like that you help me with all these children. But, if you don't mind, I'd like to keep my personal life, once and for all, out of the conversation.

SISTER MARGARET: *This* is your personal life.

SIDNEY: No.

SISTER MARGARET: Sidney—

SIDNEY: This is *your* personal life, Margaret.

SISTER MARGARET: Yes, it is. This is my personal life. You're right. And there have been nights I've wished for nothing more than someone to go home to. Someone who I loved and could devote myself to; who I could talk to about myself. A warm body to hold…to be held.

(Clears her throat at this revealing confession…)
But that's not the choice I made with my life. I went in another direction. I don't regret it. I live with my choices quite comfortably…But I'm sorry…I cannot stand by and watch you destroy what I happen to believe—what I know—is very important. Your refuge. Your adult refuge. From here. You need your own refuge, Sidney…. Love and kindness… We both made choices, Sidney. But this is your personal life too and you're killing it—

SIDNEY: No—

SISTER MARGARET: You marry a sex worker, have two kids with her, and leave her…and you want to tell me that your work and personal life are not a bit at odds at the moment?

SIDNEY: Yes.

SISTER MARGARET: And I thought you were a smart man.

(SIDNEY organizes his desk.)

SIDNEY: A smart man, Margaret, would have known that he could fall in love with a beautiful, complicated woman, marry her and give her two beautiful children, but he could not give her back her own childhood. He couldn't take away the scars and battle all the demons.

SISTER MARGARET: Did she ask you to do that?

SIDNEY: I can't battle the demons here at work and go home and do it too. I can't. There's no refuge for me at home anymore. For either of us.... It's just old wounds and shame and sorrow...that I can't help heal. I fail her daily.

SISTER MARGARET: Oh, so this is about you, is it? You think you're failing your wife?

SIDNEY: I know I am.

SISTER MARGARET: Please… Get off your high horse, Sidney. Stop acting like the only thing people want from you, and the only thing you have to offer people, is fixing them. What makes you so special? You have a magic potion, you have a wand, or some kind of super powers that I haven't seen? …No one has asked you to fix them, Sidney. Not your wife, or these girls… That's not what we're here for… We're here to give them food and shelter and aid and love and a future… That's all we can do… You think you can mend all the loss and all the scars, and you will fail…I promise. You will fail. You can't do it. All the factories in this country couldn't sew these little girls back together, make it look like nothing has changed, nothing is broken… There are too many scars and there's not enough thread or stitches to go around. We can't mend anyone back to someone they might have been, we can only hold them together as they are…wounds and all… And that's alright… That's wonderful, actually. Your wife had a horrible childhood, and it had nothing to do with you. She got hurt and you weren't there. Get over

yourself and get her some help… Send Max… Send
me… But please go home and be her friend, and stop
trying to make her all better.

SIDNEY: I don't know how to do that.

SISTER MARGARET: Why not?

SIDNEY: I don't think it's possible.

SISTER MARGARET: So you're giving up?
(She takes her coffee cup and stands.)
You and that Mr Black have a lot in common.

SIDNEY: I'm not leaving the country.

SISTER MARGARET: Worse. You're abandoning someone
who loves and needs you just because you don't know
how to be her husband without being the hero.
(She shakes her head, disappointed.)
Everybody wants to be a hero… Such a waste of decent
men.
(She exits.)

(SIDNEY tries to return to the paper.)

(TAM enters and slowly takes a seat beside him.)

*(SIDNEY and TAM sit not looking at each other. Not sure
what to say.)*

(They sit there for what seems a painfully long time.)

(Finally, SIDNEY simply grabs her hand.)

(SISTER MARGARET enters pushing a new bicycle.)

SISTER MARGARET: Excuse me, Sidney…hello Tam…
two of these were sitting outside your office.

(TAM takes a note stuck in the wheel. Reads it)

TAM: "Sidney. Please give these to Kolab and Lida.
With my thanks. To hell with Action for All…And my
father….I will return home with my head held high. At
least there are two girls in your care. (But please keep

an eye on them.) Give my regards to Sister Margaret. Go home to your wife…. Yours, Jonathon Black."

Scene 35

(KOLAB *and* LIDA *at the window.* KOLAB *holds a doll, while* LIDA *holds a map, trying to read it.*)

LIDA: Mr Webb says we are here…and that is where we were…and there are roads and houses and water here and there…maybe Yen is hiding…somewhere in between.

KOLAB: Do you think she's waiting for us?

LIDA: No.

KOLAB: Why not?

LIDA: She knows you're too young to leave. And I'm too scared.

(KOLAB *studies the doll, while* LIDA *studies the map.*)

KOLAB: I'm not too young.

LIDA: You're a little kid.

KOLAB: So?

LIDA: This is a good place for you.

KOLAB: You're a little kid.

(KOLAB *hugs the doll close, while* LIDA *continues to study the map.*)

LIDA: Look at all these roads. So many places to go.

KOLAB: What's wrong with being little?

LIDA: Nothing.

KOLAB: I can't help it.

LIDA: I know.

KOLAB: I'm five.

Scene 36

(Video:)

(Close-up of TED's *face)*

TED: Ted Thompson's going home now…going home to his wife and kids…excited about that…uh, really feel like I've seen all that I came to see…had a grand old time…really enjoyed myself…learned a lot…saw some sights…enjoyed the treasures of the land…would love to do it again sometime. Love to get to know the people.

Scene 37

(The sound of a bicycle bell O S)

*(*KOLAB *and* LIDA *enter and exit the stage riding their new bikes, happy and excited. They ride the bikes on and off stage several times until…one time they ride them on stage and they are no longer young women on the bikes—the two young women actors playing the parts of* KOLAB *and* LIDA *are now replaced by two little girls.)*

(The two little girls ride the bikes around the stage and finally come to a stop in the middle of the stage.)

(The little girls stare at the audience, then put their hands together and bow their heads in sompiah—the fore-mentioned gesture of greeting, respect, and thanks.)

END OF PLAY